I0791603

Of One Blood

How Did We Get Here?
Race is an Idea - Part 1

Yvita Marcus

BALBOA.
PRESS

A DIVISION OF HAY HOUSE

Balboa Press books may be ordered through booksellers or by contacting:

Balboa Press
A Division of Hay House
1663 Liberty Drive
Bloomington, IN 47403
www.balboapress.com
1 (877) 407-4847

Print information available on the last page.

ISBN: 978-1-9822-3032-6 (sc)
ISBN: 978-1-9822-3033-3 (e)

Balboa Press rev. date: 11/04/2019

Contents

In Loving Memory of: my husband, my cousin/sister, and my godmother.

Dedicated to our ancestors. Everything you prayed in faith for allows me to be who I am now.

Acts 17: 24-28 (esp. verse 26) KJV

[24] God that made the world and all things therein, seeing that he is Lord of heaven and earth, dwelleth not in temples made with hands;

[25] Neither is worshipped with men's hands, as though he needed anything, seeing he giveth to all life, and breath, and all things;

[26] And hath made *of one blood* all nations of men for to dwell on all the face of the earth, and hath determined the times before appointed, and the bounds of their habitation;

[27] That they should seek the Lord, if haply they might feel after him, and find him, though he be not far from every one of us:

[28] For in him we live, and move, and have our being; as certain also of your own poets have said, For we are also his offspring. (Emphasis added by me)

Acknowledgements

My parents, Ed and Mable, my sister editor / look alike Sharon and my son, James.

My daughter Jamiallah, and my sister / friends: Sobi, Trina and Courtney.

Every biological and spiritual family member, friend, co-worker, and perfect stranger who knew this project was in the making and encouraged me to finish.

Disclaimer

If you can honestly admit to yourself that your thinking and beliefs may possibly fit into one or more of the following categories I strongly suggest that you do not waste your time reading this book.

1. You believe the Creator of the universe is a figment of people's imagination and the Bible is a story book.
2. You believe you already have all the information you will ever need to get through life.
3. You believe all the information you are exposed to from the internet, social media, and news media is all completely accurate.
4. You believe there are different races of people.
5. If you are easily offended. Someone I once worked with made a great statement. He said "People love to be offended". This book has the potential to offend lots of people.
6. If you think that all the "white" people that actually have real, genuine relationships with people of color are crazy. (Some of nicest, kindest, most generous, caring people you will EVER

want to meet will be "white" or "black" or some variation of these made up terms! Hmmm…that may have offended someone!)

7. This document contains the following terms: "White people", "Black people", "Africans", "African Americans", "Caucasians", and "nigger". Since ALL of these "labels" are man-made and made up try not to be confused.

Disclaimer to the Disclaimer:

I believe there is only one "race" of people. The human race. I make an effort to treat people as individuals and not as exact replicas of every single person that looks like them.

Introduction

This correspondence came into existence because every person born has a voice, something unique to offer to the world that only they can offer. Although every word and thought in this extremely long letter are my own, I am not the only person who currently has, or person(s) from the not so distant past, who has had similar or the exact same thoughts. Thoughts about a worldwide thought "system". A system that encourages certain children to sincerely believe that their only way out of their situation is through sports, music, or becoming a criminal. Then the very same system that encourages these "certain" children in this mindset to say "Every child has the same opportunities…"

This correspondence comes after many years of research (an ongoing process), self-examination and prayer.

For those who will say this book causes division, and or I am promoting hatred, if that is what you believe, then you are correct. What each person believes will be true for them, regardless if their belief is true or false. My only desire in taking the time to write, type, copyright, and publish my thoughts is to encourage you (the reader) to do your own personal research on the current spiritual, mental, physical, social, and financial systems that exist in our country and around the world today and ask yourself "How did we get here?"

Dear Heavenly Father, I pray that I am able to complete this assignment that you have entrusted to me.

I pray it makes it into the hands, minds, and hearts of every individual it is intended to touch and change.

Father with Your words, You created this world. I pray these words You have given me will create something new for all those who read them.

My assignment.

My # 1 goal is to let all the Black people in America (and around the world), especially those born and raised in America, who know and accept that you are direct descendants of our enslaved ancestors, to be proud. Why? Because without our ancestors who were enslaved (not outsiders, foreigners, or immigrants) this country, as we currently know it, would NOT be here!!!

It is interesting how Caucasians call Black people a problem and a burden, but they would not have a country or home or business or bank account or all the financial wealth their ancestors left for them without us.

How Did We Get Here?

This is a simple, yet multi-layered question.

How did we (African Americans) get here (to the Caribbean Islands and North and South America)? Our ancestors arrived in the 1400's, originally as part of European exploration teams.

How did we get here mentally, socially, emotionally, and financially?

Try not to be offended about the whole slavery thing. Slavery was—in Europe and Africa a standard norm of obtaining and maintaining free labor. Around the year 1441 the Portuguese were the first Europeans to bring enslaved Africans to Europe to work the sugar cane plantations. The Portuguese also built slave castles, or forts that were for hundreds of years used as holding stations for millions of captured and traded Africans to leave their home and NEVER return.

The Portuguese also introduced fire arms in Africa which turned the historical and customary form of slavery between tribes into a tragic nightmare that Africans around the world have yet to wake up from. (a) & (b)

The number of Africans captured by Africans to be sold into slavery is so high that no one is really sure of the real number. In the years 1442 -1870 approximately 60 million Africans left their homeland to never return. An unknown number of kidnapped Africans died from the "death marches" (the walk of up to 1000 miles to European coastal forts), and the "Middle Passage" (the slave ship route that lasted 12 to 14 weeks at sea. The ships carried 200 to 600 captured Africans across the Atlantic ocean to the West Indies.) The Abolition Project "The Middle Passage" http://abolition.e2bn.org/slavery 44. html. There is no real way to know the number of Africans that were killed as a form of "discipline" in place of their enslavement.

It is crucial to mention that while slavery or a life of servitude was for centuries accepted as "normal", it was ONLY based on skin color when Europeans decided that they were God's chosen People to rule the world. Interesting.[1]

---

[1] (a) Clarke, J.H., 1998, *"Christopher Columbus and the Afrikan Holocaust"* pp. 93-100
(b) Franklin, J.H., 1988, *"From Slavery to Freedom"*, pp. 32-39

Race is an idea

Merriam-Webster.com.   2019.   https://www.merriam-webster.com (June 4, 2019)

"Idea"
  - **1:** a formulated thought or opinion
  - **2:** whatever is known or supposed about something i.e. a child's *idea* of time
  - **3:** the central meaning or chief end of a particular action or situation

Dictionary.com. 2019. https://www.dicti onary.com/browse/ideology (October 15, 2019)

"Ideology"
noun, plural **i·de·ol·o·gies.**
  - 1: the body of doctrine, myth, belief, etc., that guides an individual, social movement, institution, class, or large group.
  - 2: such a body of doctrine, myth, etc., with reference to some political and social plan, as that of fascism, along with the devices for putting it into operation.

Philosophy.
   a.   the study of the nature and origin of ideas.
   b.   a system that derives ideas exclusively from sensation.

Wow, 2015 marked the 50th year anniversary of the Civil Rights March from Selma to Montgomery, Alabama. For me it's so interesting that I live in America, I was born and raised in America, I'm African American (that's the label I use), I know for certain that me and all other African Americans are more or definitely just as much "American" as any other nationality or ethnic group living in this county now.

I say this with full assurance that I am correct in my assessment. I will, on these pages, step by step and line by line explain how I have arrived at this conclusion.

For the intent and purpose of stating the case of my ancestors I will use the following terms:

"Race", "White", "Black and "nigger" (please see the "Disclaimer"). I do not believe that there are or ever have been different races of people. As far as I know there is only one race of people. We call it the human race. It is amazing the tricks that the mind can play. If you tell someone something long enough (even if it's a lie) they will eventually believe lies over the truth.

"Race consciousness, and its articulation in theories of race, is largely a modern phenomenon. In the United States, the black/white color line has historically been rigidly defined and enforced. White is seen as a "pure" category. Any racial intermixture makes one "nonwhite". "One of the first things we notice about people when we meet them (along with their sex) is their race. Our compass for navigating race relations depends on preconceived notions of what each specific racial group looks (*and acts*) like. Everybody learns some combination, some version, of the rules of racial classification, and of their own racial identity, often without obvious teaching or conscious inculcation. Race becomes "common sense" – a way of comprehending, explaining and acting in the world." (c)

"Encyclopedia Britannica - Race-Human" written by: Audrey Smedley, Peter Wade, Yasuko I. Takezawa https://www.britannica.com/topic/race-human

Race, the *idea* that people are different in nature and quality based on how they look and their cultural traditions. Today's meaning of "race" became popular in the 17th century (around the same time that race based slavery became popular). From the 17th century to the present scientists have NEVER agreed on the actual number of different races. The label **"race"** has NEVER had a definite meaning.

Translation: There is **NO SUCH THING** *as different races of people…*

"When someone tells you a perfect lie, the truth is unbelievable." – Kingston Farady @KingstonFarady Twitter 5:22pm – July 2, 2015 (*emphasis added*)

(c) Aguirre, JR, Adalberto, Baker, David V., 2001, "SOURCES, *Notable Selections In Race and Ethnicity, Third Edition*" pp. 4, 6, & 7

Created Equal

I can prove that all men are created equal. It's actually very simple. All men are not created equal because it says it in the Constitution of the United States of America. All men and women are created equal because we did not create our own selves. Psalms 100:3b says, "It is He who has made us and not we ourselves…" That lets me know that I'm created equal because the Creator of the universe says I'm equal. Equal to what? I'm equal to be beautiful. I'm equal to give and receive love. I'm equal to give and receive hate. I'm equal to speak or stay silent. I'm equal to work hard or be lazy. I'm equal to be a student of life or to believe whatever I'm told by others. I'm equal to serve the Father, and my country or be an atheist and traitor. I'm equal to acknowledge every person I meet and the Creator in them, or be unsympathetic and uneducated. I'm equal to be an active participant in the direction my life takes, or do nothing and complain of my failures. Whether I do something or nothing I'm equal. I'm equal because the Father put me here on earth. It is the Father who made me, I did not make myself. That is what makes ALL men (including women) equal.

Just because we're created equal that does not mean we will have equal experiences in our time on earth. We will have equal body functions and basic life necessities. But the important thing to know is unequal experiences or unequal treatment does not mean that your life has no value. It just means you've been looking at the wrong side of the coin of your life.

"Life is like a coin: You can spend it ANY way you want, but you can only spend it once." –Lillian Dickson.

If you see your life as being always on the tail side then you just need to turn the coin over to see that your coin (your life) has a head (or bright side).

As we embark on this journey together, my prayer is that you ALWAYS remember that your coin (your life) really does have two sides. Even if most or all of your life has been on the bottom or tail side, the other side of the coin is your head. It's your head making the quality choices. It's your head believing and knowing that you are much more than what you look like. It's your head pursuing the Creator to become the person He desires you to be so that you can change the world.

In order for you to fully embrace the "I can change the world" kind of thinking you and I have to do some time travel. We have to go back to the place where someone started a rumor that one group of people is better than all other groups of people. We already know it's NOT true!

So pack your bags, meet me on the next page. You're about to take one of the most exciting adventures of your life. I promise that you will not finish this journey the way you started.

People for Profit

Yes, you are a person too. Unfortunately, your status as a person became null and void when some people realized they could make a huge profit if they pretended that you were anything and everything other than a person.

People for profit. People for property. People to work for free. This peculiar / barbaric practice was accepted because of all the profits that were being made. As long as everyone who was making money thought this business was good and profitable then surely God must agree. Besides God is the one who told us it is our right and privilege to do whatever we see fit to the heathens and savages. Did God really say that, or did someone put their words in God's mouth?

We are the ones who decide what is right or wrong, who has morals and values, who is and what is honest and true. The only thing that matters is how much money can be made. How much money did we make? Let us find a way to make more money with **these** people. *People for profit. People for property. People to work for free*—**forever.**

People for profit. People for property. People to work for free. This system of People for profit was ok with the leaders of the Catholic and Protestant church.

If the people who say they really know God, and have a special relationship with Him say this peculiar practice is "OK" then surely it must be "OK".

The following word definitions / usages are inserted here as a below the surface reminder of what these words REALLY meant / mean to all individuals who lived / live these realities, yet almost NEVER use these words (per se) to describe their reality.

Merriam-Webster.com. 2019. https://www.merriam-webster.com (4 June 2019). All.

"TERROR"
1: **a state of intense fear**
2a: **one that inspires fear: SCOURGE**
    b: **a frightening aspect**
    c: **a cause of anxiety: WORRY**
3: REIGN OF TERROR
4: **violent or destructive acts (such as bombing) committed by groups in order to intimidate a population or government into granting their demands**

"SCOURGE"
1: WHIP; *especially*: one used to inflict pain or punishment
2: an instrument of punishment or criticism

"CONTROL"
controlled; controlling
transitive verb

1a *archaic:* to check, test, or verify by evidence or experiments

b: to <u>incorporate</u> suitable <u>controls</u> in *a controlled experiment*

2a: to exercise restraining or directing influence over: regulate *control one's anger*

b: to have power over: rule *A single company controls the industry.*

"RULE"

1a: a prescribed guide for conduct or action

b: the laws or regulations prescribed by the founder of a religious order for observance by its members

c: an accepted procedure, custom, or habit

3a: the exercise of authority or control: dominion

b: a period during which a specified ruler or government exercises control

"dominion"

1: domain

2 *law:* **supreme authority:** sovereignty *having dominion over the natural world*

3 **dominions** *plural, Christianity*: an order of angels — see celestial hierarchy

4 *often capitalized, government*: a self-governing nation of the Commonwealth of Nations other than the United Kingdom that acknowledges the British monarch as chief of state

5 *law*: absolute ownership

"domain"

1lawa: **complete and absolute** (see absolute 3) **ownership of land** *our highways and roads have been in the domain of state and local governments — T. H. White b. 1915—* compare EMINENT DOMAIN

b: land so owned

2: a territory over which dominion (see dominion 2) is exercised *The forest is part of the king's domain.*

"SOVEREIGNTY"

plural **sovereignties**

1obsolete: supreme excellence or an example of it

2a: **supreme power especially over a <u>body politic</u>**

b: **freedom from external control:** <u>AUTONOMY</u>

c: **controlling influence**

3: one that is sovereign; *especially*: an autonomous state

"AUTONOMY"

plural **autonomies**

1: the quality or state of being self-governing; *especially*: the right of government *The territory was granted autonomy.*

2: **self-directing freedom and especially moral independence** *personal autonomy*

3: a self-governing state

"SELF–GOVERNMENT"

1: SELF-CONTROL, SELF-COMMAND

2: **government under the control and direction of the inhabitants of a political unit rather than by an outside authority;** *broadly*: **<u>control of one's own affairs</u>**

"COMMERCE"

1: social intercourse: interchange of ideas, opinions, or sentiments… *a negotiated peace that will reestablish intellectual commerce among them … — P. B. Rice*

2: **the exchange or buying and selling of <u>commodities</u> on a large scale involving transportation from place to place** *a major center of commerce interstate commerce*

"COMMODITY"

plural **commodities**

1: an economic good: such as *a*: a product of agriculture or mining *agricultural commodities like grain and corn b*: an article of <u>commerce</u> especially when delivered for shipment *reported the damaged commodities to officials c*: a mass-produced unspecialized product *commodity chemicals commodity memory chips*

2a: something useful or valued *that valuable commodity, patience; also:* <u>THING</u>, <u>ENTITY</u>

b: <u>CONVENIENCE</u>, <u>ADVANTAGE</u>… *the many commodities incidental to the life of a public office … — Charles Lamb*

integrated; integrating

<u>transitive verb</u>

1: to form, coordinate, or blend into a functioning or unified whole: <u>UNITE</u>

2: to find the <u>integral</u> of (as a function or equation)

3a: to unite with something else

b: to incorporate into a larger unit

4*a*: to end the segregation of and bring into equal membership in society or an organization
b*: desegregate *integrate school districts
intransitive verb
: to become integrated

"integration"

1: the act or process or an instance of integrating: such as

a: **incorporation as equals into society or an organization of individuals of different groups (as races)**

b: coordination of mental processes into a normal effective personality or with the environment

"incorporate"
incorporated; incorporating
transitive verb
1a: to unite or work into something already existent so as to form an indistinguishable whole
b: to blend or combine thoroughly

Conclusion: These word definitions / usages are referenced to explore **masses of black people's** overall experience in America from slavery to present day. Through acts of **terror, control, rules of law**, and the lack of **domain, sovereignty,** and **autonomy,** black people were and still are used as valuable **commodities** for the financial stability of this nation. Black people were not ever fully or sincerely **integrated / incorporated** into the fabric of American Society. Those of us with visible melanin were NEVER given the same rights and privileges as white American citizens. Unless lawmakers (state and federal) are willing to honestly examine all existing rules / laws and agree that most (if not all) of them need to be completely changed we will (according to history) continue with business as usual.

Created by the Creator

Africans / Aboriginals/ Native Americans are the original people on the earth. Therefore on a technicality **everyone** is African, or black, or a person of color, or a *"nigger"*? The Creator made people. He made us different, but there are no different categories of people, just people. Yes we are different, but so is every creature in the animal, insect and plant kingdoms. There are different kinds of every animal on land, in the air and in the ocean.

Look carefully at how the Creator of the universe created EVERYTHING that He created. He created a variety of every kind of animal, plant and insect. There are African Elephants and Asian Elephants, but they are all elephants. There are Brown, Black, Polar, Panda, and Koala Bears, but they are all bears. There are Lions, Tigers, Pumas, Jaguars, and Cheetahs, but they are all big cats. There are multiple varieties of domestic dogs and cats, but they are all either a dog or a cat. There are Pine, Oak, Fur, and Fruit Trees, but they are all trees. This list could literally go on FOREVER. The point I'm making is when the Creator of the Universe created this earth and every living thing that lives on this earth He made each one that is the same also very different.

Look at animals, plants, and insects, bodies of water, stars, planets, and natural food. Then look at humans. There is a wide variety of humans. There are humans who identify themselves by the continent where they are born. There are humans who identify themselves by the language they speak. There are humans who identify themselves by their family's name. No matter how we identify ourselves, when our Creator sees us He sees the ones that He calls "man and woman", "boy and girl".

Now that you have this information you can be secure in knowing that no matter who you are, where you come from, or what you have done, when your Creator sees you He only sees a "man, woman, boy or girl".

The last time I checked God creates humans. Humans don't create humans. Humans seek to control other humans and other living creatures. But God, the Creator of the Universe created the Universe and He created every living thing that lives in the Universe.

There are really one 2 types of people, good or bad. All white people are not bad, and all black people are not good. The reverse is also true, and applies to all people. All black people are not bad, and all white people are not good. (*see Journal Notes August 23, 2015*)

Well I really did just say the same thing but in a slightly different way. Yeah, it's a little Jedi mind trick that has been used on black people for hundreds of years. The enormous challenge is how generations of lies can, you know – the REAL Jedi mind trick…—how can it be reversed? Can it be reversed? I do firmly believe—with God—ALL THINGS ARE POSSIBLE.

I've been carrying this project / assignment around

with me since I was a young girl. Growing up in the housing projects in Brooklyn, NY we watched our share of television. Regular sitcoms and special broadcasts like "Porgie and Bess", "Miss Jane Pittman", "Sounder", and "Roots". I was born at the tail end of the Civil Rights movement. In elementary school during "Black History" month we were watched films about John Henry and Joe Brown. I watched talk news television with my Dad and he'd let me watch old interviews with Malcom X and Dr. Martin Luther King, Jr. I had a friend in elementary school whose Dad was ½ white or Hispanic. Due to her VERY light brown complexion she was what Black people call "beige" or "high yellow". She always struggled with her Blackness. Now me, I don't ever recall wishing to have been born white. Did I ever put a towel on my head and pretend it was long hair to fling around? Yes. But that was just a part of Black girls reality and a fun way of imitating the dominate images we saw on TV, in books, magazines, and such like.

I always knew I was black and I was ALWAYS comfortable being a black girl. Was I comfortable growing up in the projects in Brooklyn? Not always. Was I comfortable with the drama, and dysfunctional dynamics that came with living in the projects? Not particularly.

I can say gratefully that my parents were so right by teaching me and my sisters not to be envious of people who give the appearance that their lives are perfect. There is no perfect life. There is no perfect life because there are no perfect people.

I am compelled to share my passion, my process, my

project, my journey with you. The truth is my journey is the same as your journey. No matter who you are, who you think you are, or who you think you are not – my journey is the same as yours. The journey is a search for love, happiness, peace of mind, and self-acceptance.

How can we find what we are looking for if we don't know what it is supposed to look like? How can we find what we are looking for if we only seen it in movies, read it in books, or sing along with lyrics of a song?

The journey begins with me. The journey begins with you. The first step of the journey is to accept that I am and you are worthy to live a life filled with love, happiness, abundance, peace of mind, self-acceptance and self-worth.

Will you or I be required to take any action in order for this life to happen? Absolutely!

The first action is the simplest, yet holds the greatest challenge. To accept and commit to the "Change Challenge". (*See details in the "Hated and Persecuted" chapter*)

Remember, when your Creator sees you He sees a man, woman, boy or girl. If you live in America when you turn 21 years old you are considered a man or woman. Men and women are expected to take responsibility for their actions. Men and women are expected to have an education, skill or trade to either start your own business or obtain a job to supply your basic needs. Men and women are expected to be in a position to take care of children they bring into the world.

On paper that all sounds totally reasonable. However if you go back in time and see how the black family was intentionally sabotaged during slavery, Reconstruction, and up to the present you will see that reasonable expectations are not always so reasonable after all.

What black people have to know is that we were NOT a part of the "Life, Liberty and Pursuit of Happiness" equation when the Union was being established. The Europeans who settled in the Caribbean islands, and North and South America islands did not have Native American Aboriginals or Africans in mind when they were fighting the Revolutionary War (even though our ancestors did fight in the Revolutionary War). The colonists did NOT have the enslaved population in mind, as free citizens when they created the Federalist Papers, the Declaration of Independence and the Constitution of the United States of America. Black people have to know that the white people did not have us in mind because in their minds it made complete sense for them-white people- to live lives of love, happiness, prosperity and peace of mind, without being ruled by and paying taxes to the King of England. It never occurred to most of the white Colonists who were making money from having or trading slaves that EVERYTHING has a beginning and EVERYTHING has an end. In their minds Africans being slaves, servants to white people was —for them- a standard norm, and why on God's great earth would any human being—especially a white one—want to ever change that?

I do sincerely thank God for all the "white" people who did not ever agree with chattel slavery of any kind for any person, regardless of race. For all the countless white people who sacrificed their lives and the lives of their loved ones to see this "peculiar institution" come to an end. (https://memory.loc.gov/ammem/aaohtml/exhibit/ aopart3.html "Abolition, Anti-Slavery Movements, and the Rise of the Sectional Controversy")

Strange thing about the founding fathers of this country is even though they did not have us—descendants of American Aboriginals and Africans—in mind when they were establishing this nation, our Creator and true Father did. You know that part in the Declaration of Independence that says "We hold these truths to be self-evident, that all men are created equal"? Guess what? It's in the Holy Bible. Yeah, it is. You can read it for yourself in the New Testament, the book called "Acts" 17th chapter, verses 24 through 26. In case you do not own a Bible this is what it says in the Kings James version of the Bible: "God that made the world and all therein, seeing that he is Lord of heaven and earth, dwelleth not in temples made with hands; Neither is worshipped with men's hands, as though he needed anything, seeing he giveth to all life, and breath and all things; (this is the part right here) **And hath made of one blood all nations of men for to dwell on all the face of the earth, and hath determined the times before appointed, and the bounds of their habitation;**"(*emphasis added by me*)

The Bible says that God made "**OF ONE BLOOD**" all nations of men. I did not say it, the founding fathers of America did not originally say it.

You may not be a Christian, or read the Bible, that is perfectly okay. The verses do not say that God created all Christians, Catholics, Muslims, Hindus or Buddhists. It says ALL nations of men.

God sees you because He created you. Being created

by God is what makes every human being equal. I don't believe God cares about the color or our skin, or any other physical attribute we have. I don't believe our physical attributes matter to Him the way they matter to us. I think it is so strange how white people started this whole MAJOR drama about skin color. Created a whole world system that follows it, then they—white people-get upset when the ones who have suffered, clearly, the most damage—(Yes- the BLACK people) want to talk it out, over, under…! It would be quite refreshing if the damage that was done and is still currently being done to us would at least be acknowledged.

We get tired of hearing white people complain about the black people always pulling the "Race card"? Well maybe we would not have to pull the "Race card" if we were treated better.

I realize and accept that black people as a group could potentially be doing better in America. Then I'm reminded that after almost 250 years of slavery (yes there were some free black people in America during those years, and some of them were slave holders), not being treated as humans, but as chattel property, the same as a horse, cow, or pig. After fighting in the Civil War to help the Union side win, our men being allowed seats in the congress and senate (during Reconstruction), after having our own towns with every kind of business and our own schools, ("10 Thriving Black Towns You Didn't Learn About in History Class": https://atlantablackstar. com/2016/05/04/10-thriving-black-towns-you-didnt-learn-about-in-history-class/3/) only to have it all those positive gains undone because of jealousy, racial hatred, segregation, lynching, bombs, and pure **domestic TERRORISM** (PLEASE do your own research!!!). After knowing these, and many other horrific things that happened to our ancestors I realize that probably, as a people we are much further along than our ancestors could have dreamed or imagined.

13 Colonies

Now, let's look at America, or the 13 colonies. Terror by day and night

"Terror": a very strong feeling of fear. : Something that causes very strong feelings of fear: something that is terrifying. : Violence that is committed by a person, group, or government in order to frighten people and achieve a political goal. (*Merriam-Webster.com.* 2019. https://www.merriam-webster.com (4 June 2019)

How can I say all that I want to say on the matter of Black people being terrorized by white people in America when every possible thing that could or would or should be said about it has probably already been said?

The reality and constant reminders of race based terrorism is something I carry around with me *all the time*. I think all Black people carry it. I believe everyone carries it in a different way, but we all (all Black people) carry it. I carry it because I know somewhere in my past, through my parents or other relatives, someone in my family or someone that my family considered to be family was damaged by racial terror. (Visit "Slavery in the U.S." Lumen, Boundless US History - https://courses.

lumenlearning.com/boundless-ushistory/chapter/
slavery-in-the-u-s/)

In the 16th and 17th centuries the ruling elite also the law makers had to make terror, racial terror, and racial segregation legally and socially accepted rules of law in order to convince "white people", especially poor white people that black African people are meant to be, and deserved to be slaves.

The "America" we know today didn't start off as America, it started off as the 13 colonies. The 13 colonies didn't start off as colonies, they started off as territories that were ruled or governed by different European countries. Some territories were governed by the Portuguese first (they supposedly discovered the "New World") then the Dutch, the French, and ended with the British governing a majority of the territories, after going to war with the other nations over the land. The British people in the 13 colonies were citizens of England, or servants / slaves to the British King. They (the colonists) had to pay taxes to the King on all the money they made from the products and services they produced in the 13 colonies.

The amount of taxes was unfair because they were very high (does any of this sound familiar). The colonists started having meetings (today they would be called rallies and protests) because they were sick and tired of having to give a large amount of their hard earned money to some king who was on the other side of the world. They started saying things like "Give me liberty or give me death!" and "No taxation without representation!"

If any of this sounds familiar it's because if you went to school in America you had to learn this stuff.

It was / is a required part of learning American history. Someone please help me out with this. I'm ready to fight and maybe die because I know I'm being mistreated by my government, and I know I'm right in my beliefs and what I stand for, yet at the exact same time I am holding people captive. Some white people (there is no such thing as white or black people—it's all made up) will say you cannot compare the two. They will say the colonists who owned slaves were not wrong or unfair because they needed people to work their land so they could make money to pay their taxes. I would actually agree with that line of thinking. However, the way the colonists chose to get the labor force to work the land is my issue. The two main work incentives were terror by violence (the enslaved Africans were brutally beaten or mutilated in the open for all the other slaves to see), and the terror of separating the enslaved Africans from their loved ones.

Wait a minute, didn't this slavery thing start in Africa? Yes. So why are black people upset and always complaining about slavery in America?

Slavery was the number one way of having large construction projects completed in all countries of the world for hundreds / thousands of years. So why was / is the institution of slavery in North and South America and Europe such a big deal? I'm so glad you asked. It's a big deal because when the Europeans saw that the land

of North and South America was good for sowing and planting and reaping and maybe making a lot of money they killed, captured or infected with viruses an unknown number of Native Americans and never left. Hmmm...does the word "Bully" come to mind?

The Europeans originally tried to get the Native Americans (btw–Native Americans were also, you guessed it "Black"!) to work the land for free, that didn't work out. Then they tried the very poor Europeans who were looking for a way out and came to the colonies as indentured servants. That lasted for a little while but the money the white people were hoping to make just wasn't adding up especially with so much of it going to pay taxes.

Someone brought some Africans to Virginia and then it was over for the black people. We think that we are Africans from Africa. It is very likely that we are the Americans who were here before the Europeans EVER knew this place existed because they believed the world was flat or round?!). Then the white people found out that the Africans were farmers in the art of agriculture and are physically strong they started making a lot of money. Little by little all the colonists started wanting / needing Africans to be their slaves. Then they started making a lot more money and the colonists decided we have to change the laws about who could or should be a slave (and how long a slave should be a slave). The colonists didn't want the Africans to get the funny idea that they could or should have a part in the wealth that was starting to build up. The white people changed the laws so only Africans or Aboriginal Americans would be slaves in this new country that they "discovered".

When the colonists saw all of the money they were making growing sugar cane, rice, tobacco, and cotton, they changed the laws again. Now if your mother was a slave you became a slave by birth (slaves in other countries were allowed to earn their freedom with time in service, purchase, or conversion to a religious faith). Then the colonist passed a law that said if you were an African slave you would be a slave for your entire life, no way to earn your freedom. There were some slave owners who did let their slaves purchase their freedom.

The six websites below give details of how the servant / slave status of Africans in North America changed over time with the creation of injurious laws. These laws forbad Africans to own property, carry a firearm, testify in court, to have any say in their own lives, the lives of their children, or to ever be a free and fully protected citizen in this country.

"Slave Law in Colonial Virginia: A Timeline", https://www.shsu.edu/~jll004/vabeachcourse_spring09/bacons_rebellion/slavelawincolonialvirginiatimeline.pdf

"The Birth of Race-Based Slavery" By Peter H. Wood —*Excerpted from "Strange New Land: Africans in Colonial America" by Peter H. Wood, Published by Oxford University Press* http://www.slate.com/articles/life/the_history_of_american_slavery/2015/05/why_america_adopted_race_based_slavery.html

Welch - Law "Law And The Making of Slavery in Colonial Virginia", Ashton Wesley Welch, Department of History, Creighton University, https://scholarscompass.vcu.edu/cgi/viewcontent.cgi?article=1210&context=esr

"Britain's involvement with New World slavery and the transatlantic slave trade" by Abdul Mohamud, Robin Whitburn, June 21, 2018,https://www.bl.uk/restoration-18th-century-literature/articles/britains-involvement-with-new-world-slavery-and-the-transatlantic-slave-trade

"American History: Slavery in the American South", https://learningenglish.voanews.com/a/1532857.html

"Slavery and the Law in Virginia", Colonial Williamsburg, https://www.history.org/history/teaching/slavelaw.cfm#top

The changes in laws and the treatment and rights (or the lack of rights) of enslaved Africans (and all people of color) in America changed drastically in approximately 84 years. Those who changed and then enforced the laws with racial terror / violence / unimaginable brutality considered (believed wholeheartedly) themselves as decent white people and good Christians.

(This is a good time to go back and read the definitions in the "People for Profit" chapter.)

Now remember the people who owned slaves, (created and enforced the laws of lifetime generational slavery), are the VERY SAME people who started, fought and won their freedom from England in the Revolutionary war!

Did you know that twelve of the 1st eighteen presidents were slave holders and eight of those twelve held slaves captive while they served as president?!

If you ever wondered why in the world is America so confused and not able to (after all these years) get the "race" thing right?! Well there you go, America started off WRONG, went VERY WRONG with slavery for about 250 years. America tried to get it right during reconstruction, that didn't turn out well for black people. We went right into Jim Crow Segregation state laws that were upheld by the Supreme Court adding another 80-100 years of domestic racial TERRORISM. An unknown number of people (of all ethnic backgrounds) REALLY believe that Dr. Martin Luther King Jr. and the laws made or changed during the Civil Rights movement caused about 350 years of racial hatred and racial violence and terror by white people against all people darker than themselves (ESPECIALLY Black people) to magically go away.

Journal Notes

Summer 2014: In less than one year we have watched several unarmed Black men (by the way, Black people are not Black we are a variety of shades of brown, and white people are not "white" they are pink and sometimes red), get gunned down, in cold blood by White male police officers. Just recently we've had the horrific case of the white young man going into a church in South Carolina, giving the appearance that he wished to participate, only to end up killing 9 Christians who were simply having "Bible Study".

Now it's all over the news, and everyone is agreeing that the confederate flag should be taken out of all public / legislative buildings. That is a wonderful gesture and will be great if and when it happens. But let us be VERY CLEAR, taking down a flag does not completely change (or change at all) the hearts and minds of the individuals who genuinely harbor racial hatred against all people of color, especially Black people.

What you should know with confidence is this country, America, before it was called the United States of America, was built, and established on ideology not much different from Hitler's. You may think "That's an awful thing to say". It might be awful, but it's still the truth. Not only was/is the ideology almost (if not) exactly the same, but the timeline of white people in America preaching, teaching, practicing, and promoting racial hatred, almost exclusively against Black people is considerably longer than Germans outward show of hatred of Jewish people. My goal is not to diminish in any way the unthinkable devastation of the Jewish Holocaust. The Jewish Holocaust is a well-known example of how out of control a group of people can become when they follow a leader and ideology (*the basic beliefs or guiding principles of a person or group*—Merriam-Webster online) that requires: in order for one group to be up, another group has be put down, or wiped out.

Hitler was in power for approximately 12 years. In that short period of time between five and six million Jewish men, women, and children were put to death for the purpose of "racial cleansing". Why were they killed? For one reason only, because they were Jewish.

Black people have tried many different ways to convince white people that we are okay and just regular like everyone else. While we were trying to convince white people we forgot to convince ourselves that we are okay and regular just like everyone else. Actually, most Black people are not okay and regular. It's not our fault that we are not okay and regular. We are damaged by about 525 years of being terrorized in the country that we built, the country we made great. We are damaged because a real apology for causing black people so much damage will realistically, probably never come.

4-24-2015 Something to talk about:

The topic of Race and Race relations usually is VERY touchy. I think we talk about race, but rarely does the raw truth of how deep racism is embedded in the daily lives and thinking of every American come to the surface.

The multi colored brown and copper people in America don't mind talking about "Race" but in many instances we don't know important facts about "How we, got here". Not only how did we physically get here, but also how did we get "here" mentally, socially, spiritually, and economically? Becoming accurately informed of past and present racially biased laws shows the direct link to where we (American Aboriginal Africans) currently find ourselves.

One of my prayers for my family is once we know more truth about our ancestors the easier it will be for us to take courage in taking our rightful place in this country and in the world.

No matter what happened to us here in America, this place is our home and we are welcome here. In this place our great, great grandfather was beaten or killed for chasing freedom or defending his women and children. In this place our great, great, great grandmother cooked, cleaned, and worked the in fields. She also raised all the children on the plantation and had to prefer the planters' children over her own. In this place our ancestors experienced all known and unknown forms of physical, mental, emotional, and verbal abuse and miraculously survived to tell the story. In this place our ancestors will very likely NEVER be acknowledged for making America great. In this place we will likely NEVER know the meaning of a level playing field. In this place we only trust our sons and daughters to God's divine care when they are of age to come and go on their own. In this place we are continually seeking what freedom really is and able to accomplish.

We are truly welcome in this place, and we are free in this place. We are free to live, love, laugh, and cry. We have the same rights and privileges as all of God's children. The only difference is in America we have to navigate ourselves (especially our Black men) very differently from the (Caucasians / white men). We can navigate quite well in America (the same America that our ancestors built) as long as we know our rightful place. Yes, you American-African brothers and sisters, we have a place.

Our place is NOT in jail, the ghetto, the crack house, the whore house, or the gang members' house.

Our rightful place is in a courtroom as the judge, in the operating room as the head surgeon, and in the classroom as the lead teacher or professor. Our best place is in our homes and communities teaching our children how beautiful, smart and important they are to us, to God, and to their generation.

Our place is owning our own businesses and hiring our family to help make it more successful.

Yes! The VERY BEST of everything is the right place for the descendants of royalty.

August 23, 2015

All black people are not good and all white people are not bad. The reverse is also true.

All black people are not bad and all white people are not good.

What in the world does that have to do with anything?

The idea that ALL white people are good, and ALL black people are bad, and the belief in that idea has dominated and shaped every aspect of every person who has lived in America for any length of time.

What can we do? We have to know where we came from. We come from greatness in Africa and greatness in America, thousands of years BEFORE Europeans showed up. ("7 Influential African Empires" https://www.history.com/news/7-influential-african-empires, "10 Pieces of Evidence That Prove Black People Sailed to the Americas before Columbus" https://www.lahc.edu/studentservices/aso/bsu/knowyourhistory/10PiecesofEvidenceThatProve.pdf

Africans / Aboriginal Americans who were enslaved, were real people, the original humans. They had hopes, dreams, aspirations, and expectations. In the midst of seeing generation after generation of their children, grandchildren and great grandchildren living out the same fate they were handed, they still managed to believe that "ONE DAY" something would change. They had faith to believe that the Creator of the universe would see them and show them the way out of their captivity. I do not fully understand this kind of faith. It's the kind of faith that firmly believes what looks impossible is POSSIBLE!!! That's real faith, that's the kind of faith I want to have.

When I review my life and experiences I've had, I pray I've made my ancestors proud. I pray my life represents the faith they had in our Heavenly Father to put them/us in our rightful place.

I think about almost 400 years of being called a "nigger" to the present. ("Nigger: The Strange Career of a Troublesome Word, By Randall Kennedy https://www.washingtonpost.com/wp-srv/style/longterm/books/chap1/nigger.htm, "A Note on the Word "Nigger" https://www.nps.gov/ethnography/aah/aaheritage/intro_furthRdg1.htm, "Nigger (the word),a brief history" https://aaregistry.org/story/nigger-the-word-a-brief-history/)

I think about being pregnant and knowing the 99.9 percent fate of my child if he or she lived to see a birthday, and were not taken away from me. I think about living on a plantation and the master and his family and children enjoyed life and nice things and I'm treated, and considered as an animal, a piece of property. I think about being on the run, on the run for my freedom, knowing that death, or being recaptured, could come equally or more likely than reaching my freedom. But on the run **anyway**, because I know that death could not be worse than being treated as some man or woman's property.

I think about where was God who was supposed to love me? What kind of God would allow such deep, unfounded hatred to go on for so long? Being hated and **persecuted** for something I have absolutely NO CONTROL over, **my skin color**. (*Persecute: v. 1. Subject (someone) to **hostility and ill treatment, especially** because of their **race** or political or religious beliefs.*)

These are a few of the things I think about when I think about my ancestors. Most times when I think about my ancestors I think what truly amazing, brave, innovative, and creative people they must have been. To live through hardships and adversity just for being born, for being alive. Forced to believe that they were inferior in every way, at every turn. Indefinable dysfunction faced daily from the moment they woke up to the time they tried to rest.

In spite of living under such daily trauma and what some psychologist now call "racial battle fatigue", our ancestors found a way to survive. They created/invented soul food, America's original music, Jazz, and hundreds of thousands of other hidden inventions. ("List of African-American inventors and scientists" https://en.wikipedia.org/wiki/List_of_African-American_inventors_and_scientists, "14 Black Inventors You Probably Didn't Know About" https://thinkgrowth.org/14-black-inventors-you-probably-didnt-know-about-3c0702cc63d2, "List of Known African-American Inventors 1845-1980" http://johnmpinto.com/blkinvlist.pdf, "Black Inventors – The Complete List of Genius Black American (African-American) Inventors, Scientists, and Engineers with Their Revolutionary Inventions That Changed the World and Impacted History – Part Two" https://interestingengineering.com/black-inventors-the-complete-list-of-genius-black-american-african-american-inventors-scientists-and-engineers-with-their-revolutionary-inventions-that-changed-the-world-and-impacted-history-part-two)

We have ALWAYS found a way to make something from what others call "nothing", especially and including our own selves. Why? Because the people with the most melanin are God's first and chosen people. So if you hate me for my melanin you actually don't hate me, you hate the God who gave me the melanin. I was not aware, nor did I have a say in God giving me my cappuccino/coffee color. You were not there either. So since neither one us of had a say in the matter of skin color why have you hated me and all other melanin ones so?

The economic system that built this country can be seen through cloudy and rose colored glasses. Cloudy for African Americans, rosy for Caucasians. The free labor system that set everything in motion for this country to have a great name, and great wealth started on a plantation in Virginia. That plantation became hundreds or thousands of plantations across the southern states.

The problem with slavery in the 13 colonies which became the United States of America, Europe and South America, is this slavery evolved into being the destiny of the Africans / Aboriginal Americans.

The overwhelming passion (aka: greed – capitalism) for financial wealth is what drove this new kind of slave trade. The overwhelming passion to maintain financial wealth is what allowed the enslavement of 400,000 Africans to last almost 250 years, and populate to 4,000,000 Africans in America.

Slave holders and countless white people around the globe adopted the lie that slavery was the Africans gift or curse from God along with another **insidious** (*proceeding in a gradual, subtle way, but with harmful effects*) lie.

The insidious lie is that European / Caucasian people are superior and more civilized in every way than every other nationality or ethnic group, especially the African. This is perhaps, the **MOST OUTRAGEOUS LIE** that has been passed down for generations.

Yes there was sugar, cotton, rum, tobacco and other crops that were traded in Africa, Europe and Asia. But the **MAIN** source of financial wealth of a southern planter was his enslaved population of African / Aboriginal American people.

"Why Africans? / Trans-Atlantic Slave Exports by Region http://whitneyplantation.com/the-atlantic-slave-trade.html, "United Nations Educational, Scientific, and Cultural Organization: Social and Human Sciences: Transatlantic Slave Trade" http://www.unesco.org/new/en/social-and-human-sciences/themes/slave-route/transatlantic-slave-trade/, "Struggles against slavery: International Year to Commemorate the Struggle against Slavery and its Abolition" http://unesdoc.unesco.org/images/0013/001337/133738e.pdf, "The New York Times Magazine: In order to understand the brutality of American capitalism, you have to start on the plantation." By Matthew Desmond, Aug. 14, 2019 https://www.nytimes.com/interactive/2019/08/14/magazine/slavery-capitalism.html - "Slavery was undeniably a font of phenomenal wealth. By the eve of the Civil War, the Mississippi Valley was home of more millionaires per capita than anywhere else in the United States. Cotton grown and picked by enslaved workers was the nation's most valuable export. **The combined value of enslaved people exceeded that _of all the railroads and factories in the nation_.**" - (*emphasis added*)

The true force and power at the core of "Racism" / "White Supremacy" is the overwhelming passion that existed at the inception of the 13 colonies – financial wealth. Financial wealth grants the person who has inherited or earned it a position of privilege that most people think they want. Financial wealth grants the person(s) who have it power, fame, and influence.

Racism in the Western Industrial world is a house or institution and the insidious lie of "White Supremacy" is the foundation that built the house.

Racism, classism, and sexism are really the same thing. The only difference is how the people with the most money choose to use the weakest (usually the poorest) people to make more money for themselves.

Racism is a well thought out system, specifically designed to keep one group (white people) financially up and to keep another group (Black people and all people of color) financially down.

So we have a whole country that is built on division, being separate and totally unequal, violence and hatred. Then we hold up the Bible and insist that Americans are good Christians. I'm just trying to figure out good according to whose standards, and which Bible or which god are we following? The one I follow says in 1 John 4:20 *"If a man say, I love God, and **hateth** his brother, **he is a liar**: for he that **loveth not** his brother whom he hath seen, how can he love God whom he hath not seen?"* (emphasis added)

All forms of oppression are based in money, power and influence. If you own the majority of the nation's wealth then you get to decide who has political power, who owns businesses, who gets a good or questionable education, who gets good healthcare, who has money to live in certain communities, and who gets protected by law enforcement.

Every year millions / billions of dollars are spent on people of color (especially "Black" people). In order to find out what groceries, clothing, and cars we buy. What movies we watch, music we listen to, and where we go out to eat. This research is done to make sure we NEVER find out the hidden truth of our greatness by creating new ways to reinforce the insidious lie that white people are better and smarter than us. If it's true, why did white people need African Aboriginal Americans for so many years to work, not only the plantations, but also any and every possible vocation that was required to build the country? Why didn't they just do **everything** themselves? – *Pause and calmly think about that.*

Hated & Persecuted

There is documented proof that in America (in the Race / ethnicity / ancestry bias category) people of African / Aboriginal descent are the most hated and persecuted group. ("2017 Hate Crime Statistics" https://ucr.fbi.gov/hate-crime/2017/topic-pages/incidents-and-offenses under "Data Tables" open "Table 1")

Many times in prayer I have asked the Father, why so many white people hate black people for no legitimate reason? I mean how do you just hate someone that you have never met? Pure hatred for someone that has never done anything to you personally? It is phenomenal, but not uncommon. I was so determined to figure this out that I researched the origins of racial hatred. I came across a very good article entitled "The Psychology of Hatred". Hatred stems from being mistreated, suffering loss, famine, or any kind of abuse. After recovering from trauma the person who hates or who is taught to hate needs someone or something to blame whenever things in their lives are not quite right. https://benthamopen.com/contents/pdf/TOCRIJ/TOCRIJ-6-10.pdf The Open Criminology Journal, 2013, 6, 10-17. *"The Psychology of Hatred"* by Jose I. Navarro★, Esperanza Marchena and Inmaculada Menacho

Numerous white people hate black people because they are afraid of what will happen when Black people come to our senses and remember our true value and greatness according to what the Father (our Creator) originally intended for us.

I have no I idea what it's like to hate someone based solely on their appearance. There was a time in my life I did feel very strong anger and resentment towards white people. I chose to pray and be delivered from such wrong thinking. My anger and resentment were not healthy and useful tools that could cause positive change for anyone, especially me!

I believe another reason we are hated by many Caucasians is because they know all the money, prestige, power and positions they have obtained / stolen over 400 plus years of America's rise to world prominence would have NEVER happened if American-Africans (and all other enslaved ethnic groups) were not doing all the grunt work.

I wonder what would America be, where would America be, would there even be a place called the United States of America if it had not been for Africans being forced to come and forced to work here?

I believe without the Africans from Africa and the Aboriginals already in America, there is no America as we know it today.

The wealth and power gained on plantations in the South and distributed across the country and globe is a direct result of American-Africans working for almost 250 years with torture and threats as their pay. The money made from stealing, selling and reselling American-Africans plus the money that generated from the plantations and all other industries where American-Africans worked as slaves (and all businesses that profited from the slave trade, i.e. — insurance companies, and the stock market) is the same money that built America's banking system and Wall Street. Yet, in the 21st century, we are **STILL** hated and persecuted.

Over many years of watching major network news, I have seen countless cases of American-African men, women, and children (mostly men) who were wrongfully, arrested, and stopped, frisked, or killed predominantly by Caucasian police officers.

The real number of wrongful arrests and deaths is so HIGH that probably no one would believe the actual number. I know the number is staggering because I know there are thousands or hundreds of thousands of the very same cases that NEVER get reported on major network news.

Only a handful of officers in the reported cases from the last 1-5 years (2014-2019) have been convicted of a crime. It makes me wonder if there is a real way for Black Americans to be free (in the true sense of that word). I wonder if it's possible for all Black-Americans to have real justice in this country.

Slavery in America ended (in theory) in 1863 when President Lincoln wrote the Emancipation Proclamation. Former slaves were granted permission by President Lincoln to join the Union Army in the Civil War. IF the American-Africans were not allowed to join the Union Army what would America look like today?

At the end of the Civil War, in 1865 American-Africans lived as free people for 12 years during the Reconstruction period. ("Encyclopedia Britannica –Reconstruction-United States History" by Eric Foner, Aug. 21, 2019 https://www.britannica.com/event/Reconstruction-United-States-history.)

Many necessary changes in our country's political process took place in those 12 years. It is unfortunate that the American – Africans (or Aboriginals) had to see all of their gains completely reversed and ignored, especially their land promised and right to vote.

Without political power and protection of life and property as citizens, American-Africans were once again exposed to massive domestic terrorist attacks under racial segregation, also known as Jim Crow laws. ("Encyclopedia Britannica – Jim Crow law – United States (1877-1954)" https://www.britannica.com/event/Jim-Crow-law)

While it is true that victims of a crime are NOT responsible for the crimes committed against them, the victims are responsible for how they live their lives in response to the crimes committed against them. Many black people have spent too much time and energy trying to convince white people that black people are just as good as them. The challenge is how to change someone's mind who strongly believes what they believe, even when what they believe is a lie.

People of all nationalities believe the "white supremacy" lie. Many American-Africans who believe this lie hope, wish and pray that white people would value and respect them for who they are and accept and include them in their lives the way they (seemingly) do with all white people. The rest of us know better and wonder, "Who made white people our "Creator" that we should need their acceptance or approval?" *It is the Father who made us, not we ourselves.* (Psalm 100, verse 3). If we focus on getting the Father's approval then what can men do to us? The LORD is my light and my salvation; whom shall I fear? The LORD is the strength of my life; of whom shall I be afraid? (Psalm 27, verse 1). The "white" people who hate us will probably always hate us and seek ways to keep us out of the positions of power, wealth, and influence that they share and enjoy.

American Aboriginal / Africans don't realize how much power and influence we already have even though we have entire communities dealing with financial, health and safety challenges on an ongoing basis. Watch and listen carefully to TV and radio commercials / advertisements, see and hear the style of the clothes, the body language, the music, and the dance moves. Pay very close attention and discover (if you haven't already) what you find.

To all my brothers and sisters who believe they will always be in an unfavorable situation I suggest finding a way to change your thinking a little and over time your life will change a lot (I learned that from a great man of God who still preaches in Brooklyn, NY).

When you take this challenge remember all your problems / struggles will NOT go away overnight. It just means that you agree to allow the Creator of the universe to show you different ways (ways you would never consider on your own) to make your life and your loved ones lives better.

Change your thinking on where, when, and how you spend your money. Try it for six months to one year and you will discover you have money you did not realize you had. You can make saving money a game and include your family and friends, see who can save the most money in the least amount of time.

Planning is the key. We plan what we eat, when we sleep, what we wear, where we go, what we do and if we go in a group or alone. If every person with a major financial challenge would take 10-20 minutes every day planning and keeping track of every time you swipe your debit / credit card or spend cash your life will change for the better!

The "Change your thinking a little, and your life will change a lot" challenge is NOT for the faint of heart. I grew up hearing "If at first you don't succeed, try, try again." My experience is 1. See my goal. 2. Say my goal. 3. Write my goal. 4. Keep trying until I reach my goal.

Whatever I strongly believe about my life and my money goes hand in hand. Do I believe I deserve to have an abundant life with my dreams fulfilled and joy unspeakable? Whatever I strongly believe determines every big and little decision I make, daily. Every big or little decision I make determines the path of my life.

You may be the person who knows the solution for the world's plastic and air pollution problems. You may know a few people who can help you develop this solution / idea. It may surprise you what can be accomplished when a group of people come into agreement with the same idea.

Please click / visit the related 2 websites. One actual version and the other rarely told details of events surrounding Montgomery, Alabama on December 1, 1955. How the late / great Ms. Rosa Parks (seamstress and member of the NAACP), the President of the local chapter of the NAACP (National Association for the Advancement of Colored People), E.D. Nixon, Jo Ann Robinson of the Women's Political Council, Rev. Ralph D. Abernathy, pastor of the First Baptist church, Rev. Martin Luther King, Jr., pastor of Dexter Avenue Baptist Church, Rev. Elroy Bennet, pastor of Mt. Zion AME Church, Fred B. Gray, attorney, Charles Lankford attorney, and thousands of unknown, unnamed American Aboriginal/ Africans and probably also some American white citizens of Montgomery, Alabama came to an agreement to not ride the privately owned city buses for 381 days. This idea for change, changed the city of Montgomery, the state of Alabama, catapulted Rev. Martin Luther King, Jr. into the media spotlight, sparked America's well known Civil Rights movement, gained global attention, and changed the world! ("Ala. Bus boycott costs $3000 daily" By Stephanie Cornish – December 1, 2015 https://afro. com/ala-bus-boycott-costs-3000-daily/.

"Montgomery Bus Boycott (1955-56)" By Abhinav Kaul – November 24, 2007 BlackPast https://www.blackpast.org/african-american-history/montgomery-bus-boycott-1955-56/)

We cannot change or control what people think or feel about us (sometimes the people who don't like us are close family and those who say they are our friends). We cannot change our family and the circumstances of where, and to whom we were born. We cannot change what happened in the past, the circumstances and laws of this nation coming into existence.

I can change the decisions I make, daily. I can change how I live, what I eat, what I drink, how I think, what I wear, what I say about myself and others, what I watch, what I read, how I allow others to treat me, how I treat others, what I believe about myself, what I believe about the Creator of the universe, how I spend my time, how I spend my money, and how I give and receive love.

When we decide to accept the "change" challenge we will face opposition. Opposition NEVER stopped our ancestors, so we won't let it stop us! **Remember: See it, Say it, Write it, Do it!**

Not So Long Ago

When I was born Rev., Dr. Martin Luther King, Jr. was still alive. President Lyndon B. Johnson signed the Civil Rights Acts in 1964 and the Voting Rights Act in 1965. 1964 to 2019 is 55 years. The slave codes lasted from 1705 to 1865 (160 years). Freedmen's Laws passed during Reconstruction went from 1865 to 1877 (12 years), and Jim Crow laws were officially practiced from 1877 to 1964 (87 years). Total years that American Aboriginal Africans have experienced a **type of freedom** since slavery was abolished is 66 years out of a total of 314 years of federal and state legal oppression.

"A Brief History of Jim Crow", CRF-Constitutional Rights Foundation https://www.crf-usa.org/black-history-month/a-brief-history-of-jim-crow

"In 1868, with the Amendment XIV the Constitution had finally given black men full citizenship and promised them equal protection under the law. Blacks voted, won elected office, and served on juries. However, 10 years later, federal troops withdrew from the South, returning it to local white rule."

"Over the next 20 years, blacks would lose almost

all they had gained. Worse, denial of their rights and freedoms would be made legal by a series of racist statutes, the Jim Crow laws." –

"The Vault – This Map Shows Just How Divided the U.S. Was on Civil Rights in 1949, By Rebecca Onion, Oct 14, 2014 ★ 3:39PM" https://slate.com/human-interest/2014/10/history-of-civil-rights-1949-map-showing-laws-by-state.html

"A Civil Rights Map of America" (an attachment in "The Library of Congress - The Civil Rights Act of 1964: A Long Struggle for Freedom") http://www.loc.gov/exhibits/civil-rights-act/world-war-ii-and-post-war.html#obj076?loclr=twmap)

The map in the link above, provides a breakdown of all the states, public and private institutions and businesses that embraced, encouraged and practiced Jim Crow laws.

The map does not show racial intermarriage/ miscegenation was one of the main segregation laws enforced.

List compiled by the National Park Service, Martin Luther King Jr

National Historic Site

http://www.nps.gov/malu/forteachers/jim crow laws.htm

JIM CROW LAWS

"From the 1880s into the 1960s, a majority of American states enforced segregation through "Jim Crow" laws (so called after a black character in minstrel shows). From Delaware to California, and from North Dakota to Texas, many states (and cities, too) could impose legal punishments on people for consorting with members of another race. The most common types of laws forbade intermarriage and ordered business owners and public institutions to keep their black and white clientele separated. Here is a sampling of laws from various states."

Nurses: No person or corporation shall require any white female Nurse to nurse in wards or rooms in hospitals, either public or Private, in which Negro men are placed. *Alabama*

Buses: All passenger stations in this state operated by any Motor Transportation Company shall have separate waiting rooms or space and separate ticket windows for the white and colored Races. *Alabama*

Railroads: The conductor of each passenger train is authorized and required to assign each passenger to the car or the division of the car, when it is divided by a partition, designated for the race to which such passenger belongs. *Alabama*

Restaurants: It shall be unlawful to conduct a restaurant or other place for the serving of food in the city, at which white and colored people are served in the same room, unless such white and colored persons are effectually separated by a solid partition extending from the floor upward to a distance of seven feet or higher, and unless a separate entrance from the street is provided for each compartment. *Alabama*

Pool and Billiard Rooms: It shall be unlawful for a negro and white person to play together or in company with each other at any game of pool or billiards. *Alabama*

Toilet Facilities, Male: Every employer of white or negro males shall provide for such white or negro males reasonably accessible and separate toilet facilities. *Alabama*

Intermarriage: The marriage of a person of Caucasian blood with a Negro, Mongolian, Malay, or Hindu shall be null and void. *Arizona*

Intermarriage: All marriages between a white

person and a negro, or between a white person and a person of negro descent to the fourth generation inclusive, are hereby forever prohibited. *Florida*

Cohabitation: Any negro man and white woman, or any white man and negro woman, who are not married to each other, who shall habitually live in and occupy in the nighttime the same room shall each be punished by imprisonment not exceeding twelve (12) months, or by fine not exceeding five hundred ($500.00) dollars. *Florida*

Education: The schools for white children and the schools for negro children shall be conducted separately. *Florida*

Juvenile Delinquents: There shall be separate buildings, not nearer than one fourth mile to each other, one for white boys and one for negro boys. White boys and negro boys shall not, in any manner, be associated together or worked together. *Florida*

Mental Hospitals: The Board of Control shall see that proper and distinct apartments are arranged for said patients, so that in no case shall Negroes and white persons be together. *Georgia*

Intermarriage: It shall be unlawful for a white person to marry anyone except a white person. Any marriage in violation of this section shall be void. *Georgia*

Barbers: No colored barber shall serve as a barber [to] white women or girls. *Georgia*

Burial: The officer in charge shall not bury, or allow to be buried, any colored persons upon ground set apart or used for the burial of white persons. *Georgia*

Amateur Baseball: It shall be unlawful for any amateur white baseball team to play baseball on any vacant lot or baseball diamond within two blocks of a playground devoted to the Negro race, and it shall be unlawful for any amateur colored baseball team to play baseball in any vacant lot or baseball diamond within two blocks of any playground devoted to the white race. *Georgia*

Parks: It shall be unlawful for colored people to frequent any park owned or maintained by the city for the benefit, use and enjoyment of white persons...and unlawful for any white person to frequent any park owned or maintained by the city for the use and benefit of colored persons. *Georgia*

Wine and Beer: All persons licensed to conduct the business of selling beer or wine...shall serve either white people exclusively or colored people exclusively and shall not sell to the two races within the same room at any time. *Georgia*

Reform Schools: The children of white and colored races committed to the houses of reform shall be kept entirely separate from each other. *Kentucky*

Circus Tickets: All circuses, shows, and tent exhibitions, to which the attendance of...more than one race is invited or expected to attend shall provide for the convenience of its patrons not less than two ticket offices with individual ticket sellers, and not less than two entrances to the said performance, with individual ticket takers and receivers, and in the case of outside or tent performances, the said ticket offices shall not be less than twenty-five (25) feet apart. *Louisiana*

Housing: Any person...who shall rent any part of any such building to a negro person or a negro family when such building is already in whole or in part in occupancy by a white person or white family, or vice versa when the building is in occupancy by a negro person or negro family, shall be guilty of a misdemeanor and on conviction thereof shall be punished by a fine of not less than twenty-five ($25.00) nor more than one hundred ($100.00) dollars or be imprisoned not less than 10, or more than 60 days, or both such fine and imprisonment in the discretion of the court. *Louisiana*

The Blind: The board of trustees shall...maintain a separate building...on separate ground for the admission, care, instruction, and support of all blind persons of the colored or black race. *Louisiana*

Promotion of Equality: Any person...who shall be guilty of printing, publishing or circulating printed, typewritten or written matter urging or presenting for public acceptance or general information, arguments or suggestions in favor of social equality or of intermarriage between whites and negroes, shall be guilty of a misdemeanor and subject to fine or not exceeding five hundred (500.00) dollars or imprisonment not exceeding six (6) months or both. *Mississippi*

Intermarriage: The marriage of a white person with a negro or mulatto or person who shall have one-eighth or more of negro blood, shall be unlawful and void. *Mississippi*

Hospital Entrances: There shall be maintained by the governing authorities of every hospital maintained by the state for treatment of white and colored patients separate entrances for white and colored patients and visitors, and such entrances shall be used by the race only for which they are prepared. *Mississippi*

Prisons: The warden shall see that the white convicts shall have separate apartments for both eating and sleeping from the negro convicts. *Mississippi*

Education: Separate free schools shall be established for the education of children of African descent; and it shall be unlawful for any colored child to attend any white school, or any white child to attend a colored school. *Missouri*

Intermarriage: All marriages between...white persons and negroes or white persons and Mongolians... are prohibited and declared absolutely void...No person having one-eighth part or more of negro blood shall be permitted to marry any white person, nor shall any white person be permitted to marry any negro or person having one-eighth part or more of negro blood. *Missouri*

Education: Separate rooms [shall] be provided for the teaching of pupils of African descent, and [when] said rooms are so provided, such pupils may not be admitted to the school rooms occupied and used by pupils of Caucasian or other descent. *New Mexico*

Textbooks: Books shall not be interchangeable between the white and colored schools, but shall continue to be used by the race first using them. *North Carolina*

Libraries: The state librarian is directed to fit up and maintain a separate place for the use of the colored people who may come to the library for the purpose of reading books or periodicals. *North Carolina*

Militia: The white and colored militia shall be separately enrolled, and shall never be compelled to serve in the same organization. No organization of colored troops shall be permitted where white troops are available, and while white permitted to be organized, colored troops shall be under the command of white officers. *North Carolina*

Teaching: Any instructor who shall teach in any school, college or institution where members of the white and colored race are received and enrolled as pupils for instruction shall be deemed guilty of a misdemeanor, and upon conviction thereof, shall be fined in any sum not less than ten dollars ($10.00) nor more than fifty dollars ($50.00) for each offense. *Oklahoma*

Fishing, Boating, and Bathing: The [Conservation] Commission shall have the right to make segregation of the white and colored races as to the exercise of rights of fishing, boating and bathing. *Oklahoma*

Mining: The baths and lockers for the negroes shall be separate from the white race, but may be in the same building. *Oklahoma*

Telephone Booths: The Corporation Commission is hereby vested with power and authority to require telephone companies...to maintain separate booths for white and colored patrons when there is a demand for such separate booths. That the Corporation Commission shall determine the necessity for said separate booths only upon complaint of the people in the town and vicinity to be served after due hearing as now provided by law in other complaints filed with the Corporation Commission. *Oklahoma*

Lunch Counters: No persons, firms, or corporations, who or which furnish meals to passengers at station restaurants or station eating houses, in times limited by common carriers of said passengers, shall furnish said meals to white and colored passengers in the same room, or at the same table, or at the same counter. *South Carolina*

Child Custody: It shall be unlawful for any parent, relative, or other white person in this State, having the control or custody of any white child, by right of guardianship, natural or acquired, or otherwise, to dispose of, give or surrender such white child permanently into the custody, control, maintenance, or support, of a negro. *South Carolina*

Libraries: Any white person of such county may use the county free library under the rules and regulations prescribed by the commissioner's court and may be entitled to all the privileges thereof. Said court shall make proper provision for the negroes of said county to be served through a separate branch or branches of the county free library, which shall be administered by [a] custodian of the negro race under the supervision of the county librarian. *Texas*

Education: [The County Board of Education] shall provide schools of two kinds; those for white children and those for colored children. *Texas*

Theaters: Every person...operating...any public hall, theatre, opera house, motion picture show or any place of public entertainment or public assemblage which is attended by both white and colored persons, shall separate the white race and the colored race and shall set apart and designate...certain seats therein to be occupied by white persons and a portion thereof, or certain seats therein, to be occupied by colored persons. *Virginia*

Railroads: The conductors or managers on all such railroads shall have power, and are hereby required, to assign to each white or colored passenger his or her respective car, coach or compartment. If the passenger fails to disclose his race, the conductor and managers, acting in good faith, shall be the sole judges of his race. *Virginia*

Intermarriage: All marriages of white persons with Negroes, Mulattos, Mongolians, or Malaya hereafter contracted in the State of Wyoming are and shall be illegal and void. *Wyoming*

Seeing these former state laws reveals a corner piece in the "How did America, as a nation-get "here?" puzzle.

And it is no small miracle that all the laws mentioned and similar laws were officially abolished. On paper these laws were abolished. It will take a special kind of miracle to change the hearts and minds of the people who created these laws, who believed these laws were right, and taught these laws (and the behavior to enforce them) to their children, grandchildren, and great grandchildren. Did you know that the Ku Klux Klan had approximately 1 million members in 1901? 1901 is the same year that my grandmother on my mother's side was born. 1901 to 2019 is only 118 years. The history of mankind goes back over 1 million years.

All the events mentioned in this document were really not that long ago.

We can begin to see why no one really wants to talk about these matters. The truth is our great country America was built on racism. America gained its original wealth on a slave / caste / class system that was based solely on race (White Supremacy / Domination and Intimidation of the African by any means necessary). The 100 years of Jim Crow laws after 247 years of chattel slavery is said to have been worse for the African than the actual years of legal human trafficking in this country.

We can begin to see why the masses of African Americans are still trying to figure out something that maybe we should have figured out some time ago. Actually we are right on course. I mean really. You put me in chains, take me from my home, my language my culture and traditions. You put me in the bottom of a boat that is infested with all manner of disease and human waste. You put the same boat on the rough sea for 6-8 weeks or more. If I somehow manage to survive this catastrophic event, you put me on an auction block and I'm sold to another person. I become the property of another person. To do what they want, when they want it, how they want it, as much as they want it, no matter what it is, until the day I'm sold to another person or I die. The moment I decide I'm not going to obey this person who "owns" me I risk losing my life or the life of a loved one. Now take the number one and multiply that by 400,000. Then take all the above mentioned and multiply those by 250 years. Okay, so we were not being transported by ship for 250 years. Slavery was legal for 250 years, and every child born to a slave was a slave, and slaves were constantly being sold and resold away from their loved ones.

The way I see it, we're doing exceptionally well based on all the HELL and HIGH WATER the ancestors had to endure.

The real reason no one wants to talk openly and honestly about the White against Black "race" issue in America (especially white / Caucasian people), is because at some point the question of money will have to be addressed. According to white people they don't owe us anything.

There are many Black people who think all is well and fair with "race" relations in this country.

I do NOT agree. We are owed something, even if it's just a simple "Thank You" for helping make this country great. But what I (we) REALLY want to know is what happened to our 40 acres and a mule???!!!

10-29-16 Questions:

My research for this project has led to more research, which has led to a multitude of questions.

Consider:

If American Aboriginal Africans were not of value for our knowledge of farming, physical beauty, not just our physical and mental strength why did slavery last for almost 200 years in Europe, almost 250 years in North America, and over 250 years in South America?

If Europeans are the superior "race" of people why did they need or want American Aboriginal Africans to do all the hard manual labor for them, if they were able to do it themselves?

Why have Europeans spent hundreds of years trying to convince the melanin people that we are inferior and they (white people) are superior?

When did white people relieve God of His duties?

The Bible says is Psalm 100, verse 3b, *that it is God who made us and not we ourselves.*

Since we did not make ourselves when did we (people) decide that we know better than God? When did people decide who is superior and who is inferior? Who is beautiful and who is ugly? Who is smart and who is dumb? Who is good and who is bad? Who is right and who is wrong? (All based on SKIN COLOR!!!)

Maybe a better question is WHY did some people decide that other people needed to be put into boxes with labels? An even better question is why did some people accept being put into boxes with labels? Or did the people just pretend to accept the boxes and labels in order to spare their lives?

"What white people have to do is try and figure out in their own hearts why it is necessary to have a "nigger" in the first place, because I'm not a nigger, I'm a man. But if you think I'm a nigger, it means you need it". – James Baldwin

November 19, 2016

Everything in the entire universe is connected to lines. Consider these real (literal) and imaginary types of lines:

Get in line

Offline

Online

Front of the line

Back of the line

Line starts here

Finish line

Invisible lines

In line

Car line

Truck line

Yard line

Linebacker

Free throw line

Goal line

Line of scrimmage

Tow the line

Cross the line

Draw the line

Cash line

Credit line

Line of credit

Bottom line

Straight lines

Dotted lines

Crooked Lines

Cracked lines

Curved lines
Solid lines
Double lines
Line of demarcation
Freight line
Passenger line
Clothes line
Border line
Boundary line
Grid line
Property line
Skyline
Meridian Line
Wait in line
Phone line
Bus line
Train line
Airline
Cruise line
Fast line
Slow line
Down the line
Bee line
Hair line
Standard line
Deluxe line
Punch line
Line of communication
Next in line
Hold the line
Life line

Line dance
Party line
Clearly defined lines
Line up
Out of line
Main line
Hot line
Power line
Pipe line
Gas line
Horizontal line
Vertical line
Parallel lines
Perpendicular lines
Number line
Assembly line
Product line
Unemployment line
Conference line
Head line
Fall in line
Jump the line
Move the line
Prayer line
Lineage
Color line
Blood line

November 26, 2016
My "Line" theory

I think of all the lines mentioned the most important line is our blood line or is it?

If we say we believe in a "Creator" of the universe then somehow our blood line goes directly back to the one who is responsible for us being here.

Now some people believe in Evolution and some people believe in Creation. There are probably some who don't believe in either one. Whichever one you believe you have to acknowledge that we (humans, animals, insects, vegetation and such like) are NOT the original creators of life on earth.

Since we are not responsible for being here then who should have power, control, and influence? Whose fault is it that certain groups of people appear to have all power, control, and influence, and other groups of people appear to have very little or no power, control, and influence?

Is it true that the Creator made some people to be "masters" and some people to be "slaves?" Or did people decide that in order for one group of people to do well in life it was or is necessary for another group of people to be poor and miserable? Why is so much hatred by one group of another group necessary for the system of power, control, and influence to work? Why has the Creator allowed for the negative systems of power, control, and influence to go on for so long? Why has the Creator allowed hatred and evil deeds since the beginning of time to continue? Is there any way the system of power, control, and influence can change so the people who are being adversely controlled can have better lives?

Did you know that racism equals sexism, equals classism, equals the feudal system, equals the caste system? Did you know that "races" of people are not real? Did you know most of what you were taught in school and on television about which group of people have always and will always have power, control, and influence is not true? ("What Is Racism, Racism Defined" by DRWORKSBOOK http://www.dismantlingracism.org/racism-defined.html (*** *Additional must see / read links on this website*),

"The Four I's of Oppression" http://www.grassrootsfundraising.org/wp-content/uploads/2012/10/THE-FOUR-IS-OF-OPPRESSION-1.pdf,

"7 Ways We Know Systemic Racism Is Real" Ben & Jerry's https://www.benjerry.com/whats-new/2016/systemic-racism-is-real)

The above 3 links lay out perfectly the effects of long term oppression on a society.

Did you know that the people who call themselves "white" are really Europeans? Did you know that it has been scientifically proven by "white" people that the skeletal remains of the first man and woman on earth were in Africa? Did you know that ALL people are REALLY Africans? https://www.humanjourney.us/discovering-our-distant-ancestors-section/mitochondrial-eve/

So if all people in the world came from one man and one woman in Africa why do we have so many different nationalities, ethnic groups, or so called "races" of people?

If it's true that the Creator made some people better able to do all things and to be exactly the same as the Creator why do all people require the exact same things in life to survive?

If it's true that some people really are better at making rules, organizing, and governing why can't they do everything on their own without help from other groups of people?

Why was is it okay for Europeans in the "new land" to fight the Revolutionary War (enslaved Africans also fought in that war) to gain their freedom from England but not okay for American-African slaves to want freedom?

Why doesn't the American Public School system teach the truth about the Europeans claiming to "discover" the "New World" and people were already here? Why have Europeans gone to such great lengths to try to keep the "real" truth about how they came to be in "America" a secret? How can we ever know the "real" truth when we have been taught so many lies? (*Author's note: In 2016 when this journal note was written I was not aware of the information in the attached Washington Post articles.*)

"Teaching America's truth" The Washington Post -Multiple articles <u>https://www.washingtonpost.com/education/2019/08/28/teaching-slavery-schools/?arc404=true</u>

4-29-2015

When my family and I moved south, August, 2014 it was during the time that Michael Brown was gunned down by an officer in Ferguson, MO. Not long after that incident, Eric Garner in Staten Island, NY died in police custody after he had told the officers that he could not breathe. Not long after that police officers in Cleveland, OH shot and killed 12 year old, Tamir Rice who had a BB gun. Just a few months after these incidents you had a gentleman in Charleston, SC, Walter Scott was gunned down in broad daylight. Then maybe 1 to 2 weeks after that incident a young man in Baltimore, MD died in police custody. August 2014 to April 2015 is 9 months. I have listed 5 separate cases in 5 different states. All the men mentioned are dead, all the mentioned were unarmed, all the men mentioned were African American. All the men mentioned had their incident caught on video tape. (Tamir Rice was a boy with a BB gun.)

Sometime in April 2015 someone caught on tape an incident with White Americans at a Wal-Mart having an altercation with police officers. I am told that the White suspects physically assaulted the police officers YET NOT ONE officer pulled or fired his / her weapon.

Remember: All the incidents referenced were with police and individuals that were supposedly a "threat" to the police and others. All the incidents were caught on video by innocent bystanders. Yet if you reread the outcome of all the incidents you will see that only in the cases of White officers going after a Black man did the incident end with the suspect dead.

Remember: Most of the mentioned incidents got national media coverage because someone caught the incident on video. I have some questions that you may have likewise considered:

1: How many cases exist of American Aboriginal African men dying from being shot or beaten to death by the police that are not caught on video?

2: In the history of America when has any police officer (Black, White, or Hispanic) EVER killed an unarmed or armed White man and said he did it because he felt his/her life was in danger?

3: When has a white officer who has killed an innocent black citizen, gone to jail, lost his job and pay, or had to pay a fine? How can you pay for recklessly taking someone's life? (***Please reread the articles / watch the videos on systemic racism. p.68***)

To all the people, regardless of your nationality, who believe "race" is not an issue in America consider in 2003 when my husband and I had either already closed or were about to close on our first home we found a gift from the builder's welcoming committee in our garage. A hangman's noose. Yes the year was 2003, and the state was NY.

Fast forward to 2016. I'm at work having a discussion with a white co-worker, about the upcoming presidential election (it is relevant to note that in an office of approximately 20-30 colleagues / coworkers, there were only 3 people of color, including myself). She goes on to tell me that the "Black Lives Matter" movement causes division. I'm thinking to myself, WOW, then what does police officers RECKLESSLY / *intentionally* killing unarmed American-African men "by mistake" cause? What does NOT teaching our children the truth about how this country became great cause? What does the number of American-African men currently in prison being greater than the number of American-African men enslaved in the 1800's cause?

What does intentionally putting all non-white ethnic groups of people (especially American-Africans) in EXTREMELY ADVERSE situations over MANY years cause?

It causes, you guessed right "DIVISION". My research and the research of thousands if not millions of scholars worldwide, reveals that Africans did not ask to come here to work for free (indigenous American Aboriginal natives were already here and are the 1st / true Americans). We did not ask to be hated and persecuted. We did not ask to be feared. We just do the VERY best we can to live in peace. Many of us have done AMAZINGLY well considering ALL the closed doors, glass ceilings, out right HATERS and such like.

Unfortunately, some of our HATERS have looked exactly like us...

Unfortunately, many black people accept and believe the Jedi Mind trick that was used on us to keep us divided amongst ourselves. Divided over things, in the real scheme of life do not EVEN MATTER. Hair texture, skin color, where you live, what kind of car you drive, how you talk, how you dress, where you were born, where you went to school... (IT'S ALL NONSENSE!!!)

News flash to ALL black people: In case you are not aware, all white people who in the past, and currently have any racial prejudice against you, NONE of the things that you think will impress them will EVER impress them. Translation: STOP TRYING TO IMPRESS white people. They are NOT GOD, and do not have a heaven or hell to put you in.

The way I see it, the ONLY things that REALLY matter in life are between you and what you do or don't believe about God. We could go on forever and question why in the world does God let so many bad things happen to good people. After all the questions it won't change anything and it won't make God not real. So to every person who has ever or will ever deal with hardship and adversity over something that you have no control over

I suggest you choose life. The King James Bible says…
":therefore choose life, that both thou and thy seed may
live:… Deuteronomy 30:19)

We cannot change how people see us and how they
see themselves. We can't force people to be open to our
realities and admit our country is in need of more drastic
change.

The only person I can change is me. The only person
you can change is you. For me, the best and most efficient
way for me to change was by becoming a Christian,
reading my Bible, and praying for myself and others. God
made us free will agents, so each person has to choose or
not choose for his or her own self. The only thing you
have to remember is the ONLY person you can change
is your own self.

You can do research on things you have questions
about, things that interest you. You can work with your
children or children you can influence to make better
choices. You can be positive and encourage others the
best way you can. Sometimes helping is giving someone
a hug or just listening.

Our country, America, and the world are NOT
all gloom and doom. I consider myself an Optimistic
/ Realist. WHAT??? My optimistic / hopeful side is
ALWAYS looking at the good things people (white,
black, Hispanic, Asian) of all nationalities over the history
of mankind, have done and continue to do. The realist
side looks at "How long has it taken us to get where we
are now?"

My three favorite sayings are:

Nothing really is as it seems.

Miracles happen every day.

God ALWAYS has a wonderful way of working everything out.

02–15–16 The Race Question, Matter, Issue…

Can it change? Can it get resolved? How can current conditions improve? NO ONE wants to talk about it. NO ONE wants to deal with it!!!

White people don't want to deal with the "Race" issue because then they MIGHT have to admit that there is still A LOT of intentional, organized, ingrained institutional, systemic racism in the country. And if they admit it exists they will be admitting their wrongs.

American-Africans don't want to deal with it because we have shame identifying ourselves as descendants of former slaves

Of course it all goes much deeper than these surface matters. When the question, matter, or issue of "RACE" comes up there are multiple layers of things that have to be considered from all perspectives.

We could not ever truly comprehend the horrors that the ancestors endured on a daily basis. And we go around like it's no big deal. Why would anyone want to talk about those old time slavery things now? What we experience now has NOTHING to do with what happened way back then. That was before the Civil Rights movement. And the BLACK people we're somebody, we're accepted by white people, we're loved by white people. Hey, we're just the same as white people!!!! We have ourselves a Black man in the White House. He's one of us, isn't he???

It seems CRAZY that our whole country was built under the notion that people come in different categories and levels of intelligence and that somehow makes one group give the appearance of being superior and the other group who lived the same years in horror and terror and still managed to survive and NOT ALL be certified CRAZY, inferior!!!

To all the white people, to the ones who actually "get it"—may God continue to richly bless you. To the others—I'm praying for you. To my American-African brothers and sisters: if you want to have a different experience in your life you will have to do something different. If you want to break the generations of your family living in the bad neighbor, your children attending the low performing schools, your sons ending up in jail, and your daughters becoming teenage mothers… IT IS REQUIRED THAT YOU TAKE A DRASTIC MEASURE.

The best way to make an informed / drastic decision is to get as much information as possible. You have to realize that you are not a mistake. When GOD made you, you did not make yourself, nor were we created by another person. We—all humans—were created by God, in His image and likeness. If what we think and feel about each other as humans is not of sincere love for ourselves and for all humanity it has NOTHING to with how GOD feels about us. In the first book of the Bible God says when He looked at EVERYTHING He made, He said it's good. In case you are not aware, humans are part of the EVERYTHING that God made. It does NOT say that God looked at white people and said "white people are good". It DOES NOT SAY THAT!!! It says "Then God saw everything that He had made, and indeed it was very good." Genesis 1:31a

Question: If God said what He made is very good, who are we to say it's bad???

The whole "race" thing is a terrible lie that allows one

group of people permission to mistreat another group of people and then say it was/is okay… Interesting. It's just a system of corruption that allows people to operate legally doing immoral and illegal things.

In the slave system human trafficking was made legal. The sale and purchase of human beings was then and is now breaking moral laws, and human rights. But, men greedy for money and power and influence made something legal that is clearly illegal. Not just human trafficking, also rape and murder. All legal for over 400 years in this country. If a white person (especially an officer) kills a black person in 2019 what do you think will happen??? Even though the current laws say this behavior is illegal, certain people from certain groups with certain amounts of money in their bank accounts still walk away without a criminal record. WHY???? Because NO ONE wants to deal with RACE. The question of race, the matter of race, the issue of race. My husband used to tell me to stop taking EVERYTHING that happens now back to the plantation. Actually, he's right. In order for American-African people to know how we got to be so mixed up we have to go back to Africa before the slave forts and before the slave ships, and America before Columbus.

The truth is many American Aboriginal Africans will not do any kind of research to find out how truly GREAT we are. For the ones that do, congratulations in advance. Know that your Creator will be smiling on you as you embark on your life's new journey. And wait, and seek for the Miracles along the way that you will surely encounter.

Grace and Peace – Until we meet again.

References

Books

a) Clarke, J.H., 1998, *"Christopher Columbus and the AfrikanHolocaust"* pp. 93-100

(b) Franklin, J.H., 1988, *"From Slavery to Freedom"*, pp. 32-39

2 (c) Aguirre, JR, Adalberto, Baker, David V., 2001, *"SOURCES, Notable Selections In Race and Ethnicity, Third Edition"* pp. 4, 6, & 7

Websites

"Abolition, Anti-Slavery Movements, and the Rise of the Sectional Controversy" By African American Odyssey https://memory.loc.gov/ammem/aaohtml/exhibit/aopart3.html *(additional related topic links on this site)*

"10 Thriving Black Towns You Didn't Learn About in History Class" By Tanasia Kenney – May 4, 2016,

Atlanta Black Star https://atlantablackstar.com/2016/05/04/10-thriving-black-towns-you-didnt-learn-about-in-history-class/3/

"Slavery in the U.S." Lumen, Boundless US History - https://courses.lumenlearning.com/boundless-ushistory/chapter/slavery-in-the-u-s/ *(additional related topic links on this site)*

"7 Influential African Empires" by Evan Andrews – Updated: Aug. 22, 2018, Original: Jan. 11, 2017 https://www.history.com/news/7-influential-african-empires

"10 Pieces of Evidence That Prove Black People Sailed to the Americas before Columbus" by Neo-Griot – January 23, 2015 http://kalamu.com/neogriot/2015/02/02/history-10-pieces-of-evidence-that-prove-black-people-sailed-to-the-americas-long-before-columbus/

"Nigger: The Strange Career of a Troublesome Word", By Randall Kennedy, The Washington Post, Pantheon. 256 pp. $22 – Friday, January 11, 2001 https://www.washingtonpost.com/wp-srv/style/longterm/books/chap1/nigger.htm

"Nigger (the word), a brief history" Contributing writers: Phil Middleton and David Pilgrim. Dr. David Pilgrim, Dept. of Sociology, Ferris State University, 2001 https://aaregistry.org/story/nigger-the-word-a-brief-history/

"A Note on the Word "Nigger" By Randall Kennedy, Professor of Law, Harvard University – African American

Heritage and Ethnography https://www.nps.gov/ethnography/aah/aaheritage/intro_furthRdg1.htm

"Atlantic Slave Trade, Louisiana Slave Trade: Why Africans? / Trans-Atlantic Slave Exports by Region" by Whitney Plantation http://whitneyplantation.com/the-atlantic-slave-trade.html

"United Nations Educational, Scientific, and Cultural Organization: Social and Human Sciences: Transatlantic Slave Trade" http://www.unesco.org/new/en/social-and-human-sciences/themes/slave-route/transatlantic-slave-trade/

"Struggles against slavery: International Year to Commemorate the Struggle against Slavery and its Abolition" by Katerina Stenou – 2004 http://unesdoc.unesco.org/images/0013/001337/133738e.pdf,

"The New York Times Magazine: In order to understand the brutality of American capitalism, you have to start on the plantation." By Matthew Desmond, Aug. 14, 2019 https://www.nytimes.com/interactive/2019/08/14/magazine/slavery-capitalism.html

https://benthamopen.com/contents/pdf/TOCRIJ/TOCRIJ-6-10.pdf The Open Criminology Journal, 2013, 6, 10-17. *The Psychology of Hatred* by Jose I. Navarro*, Esperanza Marchena and Inmaculada Menacho "List of African-American inventors and scientists" https://en.wikipedia.org/wiki/List_of_African-American_inventors_and_scientists

"14 Black Inventors You Probably Didn't Know About" By Pamela Rosario Perez – Feb. 26,2017 https://thinkgrowth.org/14-black-inventors-you-probably-didnt-know-about-3c0702cc63d2

"Black Inventors – The Complete List of Genius Black American (African-American) Inventors, Scientists, and Engineers with Their Revolutionary Inventions That Changed the World and Impacted History – Part Two" by Susan Fourtane – May 24, 2018 https://interestingengineering.com/black-inventors-the-complete-list-of-genius-black-american-african-american-inventors-scientists-and-engineers-with-their-revolutionary-inventions-that-changed-the-world-and-impacted-history-part-two

"List of Known African-American Inventors 1845-1980" by Smith-Lenoir Graphic Creations http://johnmpinto.com/blkinvlist.pdf,

"Encyclopedia Britannica –Reconstruction-United States History" by Eric Foner, Aug. 21, 2019 https://www.britannica.com/event/Reconstruction-United-States-history.)

"2017 Hate Crime Statistics" by FBI: UCR https://ucr.fbi.gov/hate-crime/2017/topic-pages/incidents-and-offenses under "Data Tables" open "Table 1"

"Encyclopedia Britannica – Jim Crow law – United States (1877-1954)" By Melvin I. Urofsky – Aug. 21, 2019 https://www.britannica.com/event/Jim-Crow-law

"Ala. Bus boycott costs $3000 daily" By Stephanie Cornish – December 1, 2015 https://afro.com/ala-bus-boycott-costs-3000-daily/

"Montgomery Bus Boycott (1955-56)" By Abhinav Kaul – November 24, 2007 BlackPast https://www.blackpast.org/african-american-history/montgomery-bus-boycott-1955-56/

"A Brief History of Jim Crow", CRF-Constitutional Rights Foundation https://www.crf-usa.org/black-history-month/a-brief-history-of-jim-crow

List compiled by the National Park Service, Martin Luther King Jr National Historic Site http://www.nps.gov/malu/forteachers/jim_crow_laws.htm

"What Is Racism, Racism Defined" by DR WORKSBOOK http://www.dismantlingracism.org/racism-defined.html (*** *Additional must see links on this website*),

"The Four I's of Oppression" http://www.grassrootsfundraising.org/wp-content/uploads/2012/10/THE-FOUR-IS-OF-OPPRESSION-1.pdf,

"7 Ways We Know Systemic Racism Is Real" Ben & Jerry's https://www.benjerry.com/whats-new/2016/systemic-racism-is-real

"Teaching America's truth" The Washington Post—Multiple articles https://www.washingtonpost.com/education/2019/08/28/teaching-slavery-schools/?arc404=true

"Encyclopedia Britannica - Race-Human" written by: Audrey Smedley, Peter Wade, Yasuko I. Takezawa https://www.britannica.com/topic/race-human

Merriam-Webster.com. 2019. https://www.merriam-webster.com

"The Vault – This Map Shows Just How Divided the U.S. Was on Civil Rights in 1949, By Rebecca Onion, Oct 14, 2014 ★ 3:39PM" https://slate.com/human-interest/2014/10/history-of-civil-rights-1949-map-showing-laws-by-state.html

"The Library of Congress - The Civil Rights Act of 1964: A Long Struggle for Freedom") http://www.loc.gov/exhibits/civil-rights-act/world-war-ii-and-post-war.html#obj076?loclr=twmap)

"Slave Law in Colonial Virginia: A Timeline", https://www.shsu.edu/~jll004/vabeachcourse_spring09/bacons_rebellion/slavelawincolonialvirginiatimeline.pdf

"The Birth of Race-Based Slavery" By Peter H. Wood *—Excerpted from "Strange New Land: Africans in Colonial America" by Peter H. Wood, Published by Oxford University Press* http://www.slate.com/articles/life/the_history_of_american_slavery/2015/05/why_america_adopted_race_based_slavery.html

Welch – Law "Law and the Making of Slavery in Colonial Virginia", Ashton Wesley Welch, Department of History,

Creighton University, https://scholarscompass.vcu.edu/cgi/viewcontent.cgi?article=1210&context=esr

"Britain's involvement with New World slavery and the transatlantic slave trade" by Abdul Mohamud, Robin Whitburn, June 21, 2018, https://www.bl.uk/restoration-18th-century-literature/articles/britains-involvement-with-new-world-slavery-and-the-transatlantic-slave-trade

"American History: Slavery in the American South", https://learningenglish.voanews.com/a/1532857.html

"Slavery and the Law in Virginia", Colonial Williamsburg, https://www.history.org/history/teaching/slavelaw.cfm#top

The Abolition Project "The Middle Passage" http://abolition.e2bn.org/slavery_44.html